How to launch your own company

A Comprehensive Guide to Success

OG Logo

GAIN ACCESS TO MORE BOOKS FROM ME

Table of Contents:

Introduction

Welcome to the world of entrepreneurship! Aspiring business owners like yourself possess an extraordinary vision, ambition, and drive to make a lasting impact. You understand that launching your own company is not only about financial gains but also about creating something meaningful and fulfilling.

Setting foot on the path of entrepreneurship can be both thrilling and overwhelming. It requires a unique skill set, extensive knowledge, and a strategic approach to navigate through the challenges that lie ahead. However, fear not, for this comprehensive guide will equip you with all the essential tools, insights, and resources needed to confidently launch your own company.

But before we delve into the depths of this book, let us share with you a short story that unveils the transformative power this guide possesses.

Short Story: The Remarkable Transformation

Meet Emily, an enthusiastic young professional searching for a meaningful way to channel her creativity and passion for sustainable fashion. Stumbling upon this book, "How to launch your own company," on one of her online ventures, she found herself drawn in by its promises of guidance and support.

Intrigued, Emily decided to take a leap of faith and invested in this comprehensive guide. As she eagerly began reading, she found herself captivated by the practical advice, insightful anecdotes, and step-by-step strategies provided within the pages. Emily realized that this was not just another generic self-help book, but rather a goldmine of knowledge tailored specifically for aspiring entrepreneurs like herself.

Applying the principles and recommendations from the book, Emily embarked on her entrepreneurial journey. Armed with newfound confidence, she meticulously crafted a business plan, sought funding from investors, built a dedicated team, and developed a unique brand identity. Though challenges arose along the way, Emily remained tenacious, leveraging the wisdom and tools gained from this guide to overcome obstacles and learn from her mistakes.

Months turned into years, and Emily's vision materialized before her eyes. Her sustainable fashion company not only achieved financial success but also created a positive social impact, inspiring others to embrace eco-friendly fashion choices. She now stands as a testament to the power of this comprehensive guide, and her story serves as a testament to the transformative potential it holds for every aspiring entrepreneur who embarks on their own journey.

Now, it is your turn to embark on your remarkable journey towards launching your own company. Whether you are driven by a passion to solve a problem, a desire to shape the industry, or an unyielding determination to make a difference, this book is here to assist you in realizing your dreams.

Within these pages, you will find a comprehensive roadmap that will guide you through every step of the entrepreneurial process. From refining your business idea to creating a solid business plan, from attracting investors to marketing your products or services, this guide covers it all. Moreover, it provides invaluable insights from successful entrepreneurs who have walked this path before you, offering their wisdom, advice, and cautionary tales.

Remember, launching your own company is not merely about making money. It's about creating something that resonates with your values, fulfills your purpose, and brings about positive change. This book will not only empower you with the necessary knowledge and skills but also inspire you to embrace the challenges and persevere when the going gets tough.

So, let our journey together commence. Open your mind, prepare to be challenged, and embrace the opportunities that lie ahead. Your dreams of launching your own company are within reach, and this guide will serve as your trusted companion along the way. Let's turn your vision into a reality and make your entrepreneurial aspirations soar to new heights.

Chapter 1

Defining Your Vision

One crucial aspect of personal and professional success lies in defining and clarifying your vision. By delving into your passion, expertise, and setting long-term goals, you can develop a clear path towards achievement. Further, building a strong mission statement serves as a guiding compass, aiding in decision-making processes and ensuring alignment with your overall vision. This comprehensive content will shed light on each aspect, guiding you towards defining your vision with clarity and purpose.

Identifying Your Passion and Expertise:

To define your vision, it is vital to uncover your true passions and areas of expertise. Reflect on what drives you, what ignites that fire within. Delving into your passions will help you identify the specific fields or industries that resonate with you the most. Interests that evoke curiosity, joy, and a sense of purpose are often indicative of one's passion.

Simultaneously, assess your expertise. What skills, knowledge, or experiences do you possess that set you apart? Identifying your expertise encourages you to embrace your unique strengths, enabling you to excel in your chosen path. Combining your passions and expertise provides a solid foundation for defining a vision that perfectly aligns with who you are and what you can offer.

Setting Long-term Goals and Objectives:

Once you have identified your passion and expertise, the next step is to set long-term goals and objectives that will guide you towards your vision. Long-term goals are the milestones you aim to achieve over an extended period, often spanning several years. These goals should be specific, measurable, attainable, relevant, and time-bound (SMART goals) to effectively chart your course.

Consider where you envision yourself in the future and break down your goals into smaller, manageable objectives. These objectives act as stepping stones towards your long-term goals, ensuring that you are consistently progressing and moving forward. Regularly review and adjust your goals and objectives as needed, allowing flexibility to adapt to changing circumstances while remaining focused on the overall vision.

Building a Strong Mission Statement:

To solidify your vision, crafting a robust mission statement is essential. A mission statement summarizes the purpose, values, and goals of an individual or organization. It serves as a guidepost, clarifying the fundamental principles that drive decision-making and actions.

When building your mission statement, reflect on your vision and the core principles that define it. Consider your values, what you aspire to achieve, and how you aim to make a positive impact. Craft a concise and compelling statement that clearly communicates your purpose and resonates with your core beliefs and aspirations. This mission statement will provide you with a guiding light as you navigate through various opportunities and challenges along your journey to success.

Remember, your mission statement should be authentic and transparent. It should reflect your passion, expertise, long-term goals, and the positive change you wish to create in the world. Regularly revisit and refine your mission statement to ensure it remains relevant and aligned with your evolving vision.

Defining your vision requires a thoughtful exploration of your passion, expertise, and long-term goals while building a strong mission statement to guide your actions. By identifying your passions and expertise, setting meaningful long-term goals, and developing a clear mission statement, you will be equipped with a roadmap towards realizing your vision. Embrace the process, stay true to yourself, and let your vision ignite the path to a fulfilling and successful life journey.

Chapter 2

Conducting Market Research

Market research is a crucial process for businesses of all sizes, helping them make informed decisions and stay competitive in today's fast-paced marketplace. It involves gathering and analyzing data related to market trends, consumer demographics, competitor analysis, industry landscape, and identifying target audience and customer segments. This comprehensive guide will discuss each of these aspects in detail.

1. Understanding Market Trends and Demographics:

To conduct effective market research, it is essential to have a clear understanding of the current and emerging market trends. This entails identifying changes in consumer preferences, buying patterns, and market dynamics to predict future demand. Additionally, analyzing demographic factors such as age, gender, income level, and geographic location helps businesses tailor their products or services to meet the needs and preferences of specific target market segments.

2. Analyzing Competitors and Industry Landscape:

Analyzing competitors and understanding the broader industry landscape is critical for gauging market potential and gaining a competitive advantage. By identifying direct and indirect competitors, businesses can assess their strengths, weaknesses, pricing strategies, marketing techniques, and market share. This analysis enables businesses to position themselves effectively, identify gaps in the market, and differentiate their offerings to attract and retain customers.

3. Identifying Target Audience and Customer Segments:

Identifying the target audience and customer segments is fundamental for successful marketing campaigns and product development. This involves researching and segmenting the market based on factors such as age, gender, income, location, interests, and buying behavior. By understanding the specific needs, preferences, and purchasing power of different customer segments, businesses can tailor their marketing messages, product features, and pricing strategies to maximize customer appeal and drive sales.

Conducting market research is an indispensable process that enables businesses to gain a deep understanding of market trends and demographics, analyze competitors and the industry landscape, and identify the target audience and customer segments. By leveraging this valuable information, businesses can make informed decisions, develop effective marketing strategies, and stay ahead in today's competitive marketplace.

Chapter 3

Developing a Business Plan

Developing a comprehensive business plan is crucial for any aspiring entrepreneur or existing business owner looking to grow their enterprise. A well-crafted business plan serves as a roadmap that outlines the steps, strategies, and targets required for achieving long-term success. In this article, we will focus on the key elements of a business plan, which include outlining the business structure and legal requirements, creating a unique value proposition, crafting a marketing and sales strategy, and establishing financial projections and budgeting.

The first step in developing a business plan is to outline the business structure and legal requirements. This entails determining the legal structure of the business, such as a sole proprietorship, partnership, limited liability company (LLC), or corporation. Each structure has its own set of legal requirements and implications for taxes, liability, and ownership. It is crucial to research and understand these legal requirements to ensure compliance and minimize potential risks.

Creating a unique value proposition is the next vital component of a business plan. This involves identifying what sets your product or service apart from competitors and why customers would choose your offering over others in the market. A strong value proposition reinforces your target market's perception of your business's unique advantage and helps attract and retain customers.

Understanding your target audience's needs, preferences, and pain points is essential for crafting a compelling value proposition.

Crafting a marketing and sales strategy is another crucial aspect of a business plan. This entails determining the most effective marketing channels and tactics to reach and engage your target audience. It also involves developing a pricing strategy, determining distribution channels, and outlining promotional activities and campaigns. A well-defined marketing and sales strategy helps drive brand awareness, generate leads, and convert them into customers.

Establishing financial projections and budgeting is the final key element of a business plan. This involves forecasting revenue and expenses, projecting cash flow, and setting financial goals and milestones. Financial projections provide a realistic view of the business's potential for profitability and sustainability. A detailed budget ensures that resources are allocated efficiently and allows for monitoring and adjusting financial performance over time.

Developing a comprehensive business plan requires careful consideration of various elements. Outlining the business structure and legal requirements ensures compliance and minimizes risks. Creating a unique value proposition helps differentiate the business from competitors and attract customers. Crafting a marketing and sales strategy drives brand awareness, generates leads, and increases sales.

Establishing financial projections and budgeting provides a realistic view of the business's financial performance and goals. By addressing these key components, a well-developed business plan paves the way for success and helps entrepreneurs and business owners navigate the challenges and opportunities that lie ahead.

Chapter 4

Building Your Team

Defining Roles and Responsibilities:

One of the crucial steps in building a successful team is clearly defining the roles and responsibilities of each team member. This ensures everyone knows their tasks, helps to avoid misunderstandings, and promotes collaboration. Clearly outlining expectations and deliverables enables team members to focus on their strengths and contribute their best to the team's overall success. A well-defined structure also helps in identifying gaps in skills or knowledge, offering an opportunity to address them effectively.

Hiring the Right Talent:

While defining roles is important, it is equally essential to bring on board the right talent to fill those roles. Hiring employees with the right skills, experience, and cultural fit is crucial for the team's success. This involves not only assessing technical capabilities but also evaluating their mindset, attitude, and work ethic to ensure they align with the organization's values and goals. Investing time and effort into the hiring process can save significant resources in the long run by reducing turnover and fostering a more productive work environment.

Fostering a Positive Organizational Culture:

Creating a positive organizational culture is a key aspect of building a strong team. A supportive and inclusive culture encourages open communication, trust, and collaboration among team members. It promotes creativity, engagement, and employee satisfaction, fostering a sense of belonging and motivation. Leaders play a vital role in cultivating this culture by setting an example, promoting transparency, and recognizing and rewarding achievements. Encouraging teamwork, celebrating diversity, and providing opportunities for personal and professional growth are essential for creating a positive work environment that empowers team members to excel and contribute their best.

Developing Leadership Skills:

Building a successful team involves developing leadership skills among team members. Strong leadership is vital for guiding and inspiring the team towards achieving its goals. Investing in leadership development programs, coaching, and continuous learning opportunities can help team members enhance their leadership capabilities. Effective leaders are able to motivate and empower their team, provide clear direction, delegate tasks efficiently, and resolve conflicts constructively. Developing leadership skills within the team not only enhances overall team performance but also prepares individuals for future leadership positions, fostering growth and succession planning within the organization.

Building a successful team requires attention to defining roles and responsibilities, hiring the right talent, fostering a positive organizational culture, and developing leadership skills. By focusing on these key aspects, organizations can create a cohesive and high-performing team that is capable of overcoming challenges, achieving goals, and driving long-term success.

Chapter 5

Securing Funding

Securing funding for your business is a crucial step towards its success and growth. There are several options available to entrepreneurs when it comes to financing their ventures. In this comprehensive content, we will explore four different methods: self-funding and bootstrapping, seeking investors and venture capital, applying for small business loans or grants, and utilizing crowdfunding and crowdsourcing.

1. Self-Funding and Bootstrapping:

Self-funding involves using personal savings, assets, or credit to finance your business. It allows you to maintain control and ownership without involving external parties. Bootstrapping, on the other hand, refers to starting and running your business with limited resources and minimal external assistance. It requires resourcefulness, careful cost management, and an emphasis on generating revenue early on.

2. Seeking Investors and Venture Capital:

If your business has significant growth potential, seeking investors or venture capitalists might be a suitable option. Investors provide capital in exchange for equity or ownership in your company, while venture capitalists typically invest in high-growth startups. Before approaching potential investors, it's essential to have a well-formed business plan, clearly articulated vision, and a compelling pitch.

3. Applying for Small Business Loans or Grants:

Small business loans and grants can provide much-needed capital without giving up equity in your company. Loans are typically obtained from banks or financial institutions and require repayment with interest over a specific period. Grants, on the other hand, are non-repayable funds given by government agencies, foundations, or corporations to support businesses in specific industries or regions. Research the eligibility criteria and carefully prepare your application to increase your chances of securing these funding options.

4. Crowdfunding and Crowdsourcing:

Crowdfunding has gained popularity as a modern method of raising funds. It involves reaching out to a large number of individuals through online platforms and pitching your business idea or project. In return for their investment, these individuals receive rewards, equity, or pre-purchased products or services. Crowdsourcing, on the other hand, involves leveraging the collective knowledge, skills, and resources of a virtual community to fund and support your project. This method can be valuable for gathering feedback, generating ideas, and finding potential collaborators.

Regardless of the funding option you choose, it is essential to thoroughly research and understand the terms, obligations, and risks involved.

Securing funding is a critical step towards achieving your business goals, but it's equally important to have a solid business plan, a unique value proposition, and a relentless drive to succeed.

With the right funding and strategic planning, you can position your business for growth, innovation, and long-term success.

Chapter 6

Establishing Legal and Regulatory Compliance

In today's complex business landscape, it is crucial for entrepreneurs and businesses to ensure they comply with various legal and regulatory requirements. To safeguard their interests and build a solid foundation, businesses must focus on key areas such as registering their business, obtaining licenses, understanding intellectual property rights, complying with tax and employment laws, and protecting customer data and privacy.

Registering Your Business and Obtaining Licenses:

The first step in establishing legal compliance is to register your business. Depending on the jurisdiction and the type of business entity, this process may include registering with relevant authorities, such as company registries, tax departments, or professional bodies. By formalizing your business, you gain legal recognition and can access various benefits such as liability protection and tax advantages.

Additionally, certain industries may require obtaining specific licenses or permits. Examples include liquor licenses for restaurants, medical licenses for healthcare providers, or construction permits for builders. Ensuring compliance with these licensing requirements not only prevents penalties and legal issues but also builds trust among customers and partners.

Understanding Intellectual Property Rights:

Intellectual property (IP) is a valuable asset for businesses as it defines their uniqueness and sets them apart from competitors. It is imperative to understand and protect your IP rights to avoid infringement, unauthorized use, or misappropriation. Copyrights, patents, trade secrets, and trademarks are all included in this. Consulting with an IP attorney is advisable to evaluate your company's IP assets, register trademarks and copyrights, file for patents when necessary, and establish strategies to defend your IP rights.

Complying with Tax and Employment Laws:

Compliance with tax laws is essential for businesses to avoid legal issues and hefty fines. Understanding your tax obligations, such as income tax, sales tax, and payroll taxes, is crucial. Consult with tax professionals or accountants to ensure accurate record-keeping, timely payments, and proper filing of tax returns.

Similarly, compliance with employment laws is of utmost importance to protect both the business and its employees. Familiarize yourself with local labor laws to ensure fair employment practices, proper classification of workers, adherence to minimum wage and overtime regulations, and provision of a safe working environment. Having employment contracts, employee handbooks, and policies in place can greatly assist in establishing compliance.

Protecting Customer Data and Privacy:

In today's digital era, protecting customer data and privacy has become increasingly important. Businesses must adopt robust data protection measures to safeguard sensitive customer information from unauthorized access, data breaches, or cyber threats. This includes implementing secure IT infrastructure, utilizing encryption methods, regularly updating software, and establishing data protection policies and procedures.

Compliance with privacy laws, such as the General Data Protection Regulation (GDPR) in the European Union, is also crucial. This includes obtaining explicit consent from individuals for collecting and using their personal data, providing transparency in data handling practices, and allowing individuals to exercise their rights related to their personal information.

By prioritizing the establishment of legal and regulatory compliance in these areas, businesses can not only mitigate legal risks and potential penalties but also build a reputation for trustworthiness and ethical practices. Compliance should be an ongoing process, with regular reviews and updates to adapt to changing laws and regulations to ensure long-term success and sustainability.

Chapter 7

Setting Up Operations and Infrastructure

Setting up operations and infrastructure is a critical component of any business establishment. It involves various aspects such as selecting the right location and office space, choosing suitable business tools and technologies, establishing a supply chain and inventory management system, and implementing operational systems for efficiency. This comprehensive content will delve into each of these areas in order to provide valuable insights and guidance for a successful setup.

1. Choosing the Right Location and Office Space:

Selecting the right location is crucial for any business as it can directly impact its success. Factors such as proximity to target market, accessibility, availability of resources, and cost-effectiveness should be taken into consideration. Additionally, the office space should be chosen based on the specific needs and requirements of the business, including scalability, safety, and amenities available.

2. Selecting Business Tools and Technologies:

In today's digital age, having the right business tools and technologies is essential for efficient operations. Be it software solutions, communication systems, or project management tools, careful consideration should be given to selecting tools that align with the business needs and goals.

Researching and comparing various options, including their features, pricing, and integration capabilities, will help ensure the right choices are made.

3. Establishing Supply Chain and Inventory Management:

Efficient supply chain and inventory management are crucial for businesses that deal with physical products. Establishing a reliable supply chain involves selecting trustworthy suppliers, negotiating favorable terms, and ensuring timely delivery of raw materials or finished goods. Implementing inventory management systems helps businesses maintain optimal inventory levels, avoid stockouts or overstocking, and streamline ordering and fulfillment processes.

4. Implementing Systems for Operations and Efficiency:

Implementing systems and processes that promote operational efficiency is key to running a successful business. This includes setting up clear workflows and standard operating procedures, automating repetitive tasks, and utilizing technology to streamline operations. By identifying bottlenecks, measuring performance, and continuously improving processes, businesses can optimize productivity, minimize errors, and reduce costs.

Setting up operations and infrastructure requires careful planning and decision-making. Choosing the right location and office space, selecting suitable business tools and technologies, establishing an efficient supply chain and inventory management system, and implementing systems for operations and efficiency are all crucial steps in this process.

By giving due consideration to these areas, businesses can create a strong foundation for success and ensure smooth operations in the long run.

Chapter 8

Developing Your Brand Identity

Creating a Memorable Brand Name and Logo:

One of the first steps in developing your brand identity is creating a memorable brand name and logo. Your brand name should be unique, easy to pronounce, and relevant to your industry or target audience. Try performing market research and holding brainstorming meetings to help you come up with a name that appeals to your target audience.

Simultaneously, designing a visually appealing logo is essential for brand recognition. Your brand's principles and personality should be portrayed visually in your logo. Choose colors, fonts, and imagery that align with your brand's message. Remember, simplicity is key as it allows for easier recognition and scalability across different platforms.

Crafting Brand Messaging and Value Proposition:

Once you have established your brand name and logo, it is vital to craft a strong brand messaging and value proposition. Your messaging should clearly communicate your brand's mission, vision, and values. Outline the unique selling points of your products or services and demonstrate how they provide value to your customers. Focus on what sets your brand apart from the competition.

To create an impactful brand messaging, identify your target audience and understand their pain points, desires, and aspirations. Tailor your messaging to resonate with them and evoke an emotional connection. Consistently communicate this messaging across all marketing collaterals and touchpoints to reinforce your brand identity.

Designing a Consistent Visual Identity:

Having a consistent visual identity is crucial for building brand recognition and establishing a cohesive brand image. This includes the design elements such as colors, typography, imagery, and overall aesthetics used across your website, social media profiles, packaging, and other brand assets.

Create brand guidelines that outline the rules for using your brand's visual elements, ensuring consistency in their application. Use consistent color schemes and fonts that align with your brand's personality and values. Incorporate your logo and brand name into all visual assets to create a unified visual identity.

Building Brand Awareness and Engagement:

Once you have established a strong brand identity, it's time to build awareness and engage with your target audience. Utilize various marketing channels and tactics to reach out to your potential customers. This can include social media marketing, content marketing, influencer collaborations, email marketing, and traditional advertising.

Creating captivating content that aligns with your brand messaging will help attract and engage your audience. Use storytelling techniques to convey your brand's values and connect with your customers on an emotional level. Encourage user-generated content and actively participate in conversations on social media to foster engagement and build a community around your brand.

Regularly analyze data and metrics to measure the effectiveness of your brand awareness and engagement efforts. This will assist you in determining which tactics are effective and which require improvement.

Adapt your approach accordingly to optimize your brand's reach and impact.

Developing your brand identity is a multi-faceted process that involves creating a memorable brand name and logo, crafting compelling brand messaging and value proposition, designing a consistent visual identity, and building brand awareness and engagement. By paying attention to these key elements, you can establish a strong and recognizable brand that resonates with your target audience, differentiates you from competitors, and drives long-term success for your business.

Chapter 9

Launching Your Product or Service

When it comes to introducing your product or service to the market, a well-planned launch strategy is essential for success. This comprehensive guide will walk you through the key steps in launching your product or service, from developing a successful launch strategy to generating buzz and excitement.

1. Developing a Successful Product Launch Strategy:

Before diving into the launch process, it is crucial to outline a solid strategy. Start by identifying your target market, understanding their needs and preferences, and conducting market research to assess demand. This will help you determine how to position your product or service in the market and create a unique selling proposition. Additionally, set clear goals and objectives for your launch, such as sales targets or market penetration. A well-defined strategy will serve as a roadmap for all subsequent actions.

2. Establishing Pricing and Packaging:

Determining the right price for your product or service is crucial, as it directly affects its perceived value and market competitiveness. Conduct a competitive analysis to understand the pricing landscape and set a price that aligns with your target audience's expectations. Take into account elements like perceived value, intended profit margins, and production expenses. Additionally, packaging plays a significant role in attracting customers, so invest time and resources in designing appealing and informative packaging that reflects your brand identity.

3. Implementing Effective Distribution Channels:

Selecting the right distribution channels is vital for reaching your target audience efficiently. Consider both online and offline channels, such as e-commerce platforms, retail stores, or partnerships with industry influencers. Evaluate the strengths and weaknesses of each channel and choose the ones that align with your target audience's preferences and purchasing behavior. Build strong relationships with distributors or retailers to ensure the smooth flow of your product or service to the market.

4. Creating Buzz and Generating Excitement:

To create a successful launch, generating buzz and excitement around your product or service is crucial. Start by crafting compelling marketing messages that highlight the unique features and benefits of your offering. Utilize various marketing channels, such as social media, email marketing, PR campaigns, and influencer collaborations, to create anticipation and drive awareness. Consider implementing pre-launch activities such as teaser campaigns, limited-time offers, or exclusive sneak peeks to build excitement among your target audience.

Launching your product or service requires careful planning and execution. By developing a successful launch strategy, establishing the right pricing and packaging, implementing effective distribution channels, and creating buzz and excitement, you can position your offering for success in the market. Remember to continuously monitor and evaluate your launch efforts to make adjustments and optimize your strategy for maximum impact.

Chapter 10

Marketing and Promoting Your Company

Crafting a Comprehensive Marketing Plan:

In order to effectively market and promote your company, it is crucial to have a comprehensive marketing plan in place. This plan should outline your target audience, marketing goals, strategies, and tactics to be utilized. By thoroughly understanding your target audience, you can tailor your marketing efforts to effectively reach and engage with them. Additionally, a well-crafted marketing plan will allow you to allocate resources efficiently and make informed decisions when it comes to promoting your company.

Utilizing Digital Marketing Channels:

With the rise of technology, digital marketing channels have become an essential component of marketing and promoting a company. These channels include websites, search engine optimization (SEO), email marketing, content marketing, and pay-per-click advertising (PPC), among others. Utilizing these channels allows you to reach a wider audience, increase brand visibility, promote products or services, and generate leads. By harnessing the power of digital marketing, you can effectively target and engage with your desired audience.

Leveraging Social Media and Influencer Marketing:

Social media platforms have revolutionized the way companies market and promote their products or services. With billions of users worldwide, platforms such as Facebook, Instagram, Twitter, and LinkedIn provide a unique opportunity to connect with potential customers. By creating compelling and engaging content, establishing a strong brand presence, and interacting with your audience, social media can help you build brand loyalty and increase your customer base.

Influencer marketing has also emerged as a powerful tool for promoting companies. Influencers, who possess a significant following and influence within a specific niche, can help promote your products or services to their audience. By partnering with relevant influencers, you can leverage their credibility and reach to raise awareness and generate interest in your company.

Measuring Marketing Effectiveness and ROI:

To ensure that your marketing efforts are successful, it is essential to measure their effectiveness and return on investment (ROI). This can be done by analyzing key performance indicators (KPIs) such as website traffic, conversion rates, social media engagement, and sales revenue. By tracking these metrics, you can identify which marketing strategies and tactics are working and which ones need improvement. This data-driven approach will enable you to optimize your marketing campaigns, allocate resources effectively, and achieve a higher ROI.

Marketing and promoting your company require a comprehensive approach that encompasses crafting a detailed marketing plan, utilizing digital marketing channels, leveraging social media and influencer marketing, and measuring the effectiveness and ROI of your efforts.

By implementing these strategies, you can increase brand awareness, engage with your target audience, and drive sales growth for your company.

Chapter 11

Building Customer Relationships

Building strong customer relationships is vital for businesses to thrive in today's competitive market. By focusing on four key strategies, businesses can effectively build and maintain strong connections with their customers: providing exceptional customer service, implementing customer relationship management (CRM) systems, collecting and analyzing customer feedback, and creating customer loyalty and retention programs.

First and foremost, providing exceptional customer service should be at the forefront of every business's strategy. By going above and beyond to meet and exceed customer expectations, businesses can foster positive experiences and build long-lasting relationships. This includes resolving issues promptly, being readily available to address concerns, and ensuring a smooth and pleasant customer journey throughout every interaction.

Implementing CRM systems is another crucial aspect of building customer relationships. These systems enable businesses to effectively manage and nurture relationships at every stage, from prospecting to post-sale support. CRM systems provide a centralized database for storing and managing customer information, allowing businesses to better understand their customers' needs and preferences. This data can be leveraged to tailor marketing campaigns, personalize communications, and ultimately, deliver a more personalized and relevant experience to customers.

Collecting and analyzing customer feedback is essential for businesses looking to enhance their relationships with customers. By actively seeking feedback through surveys, feedback forms, or social media channels, businesses can gain valuable insights into customer satisfaction, preferences, and areas for improvement. Analyzing this feedback allows businesses to identify patterns and trends, helping them make data-driven decisions to enhance their products, services, and overall customer experience.

In addition to gathering feedback, businesses should also prioritize creating customer loyalty and retention programs. These programs aim to reward and incentivize customers for their continued support and loyalty. This can be done through exclusive discounts, loyalty points, personalized offers, or special events. By implementing these programs, businesses can not only encourage repeat purchases but also foster a sense of belonging and appreciation among their customers.

Building strong customer relationships requires an ongoing commitment to providing exceptional customer service, leveraging CRM systems, collecting feedback, and implementing loyalty programs. It is crucial to remember that customer relationships are not built overnight but require consistent efforts and a customer-centric mindset. By investing in building long-term relationships with their customers, businesses can enjoy increased customer satisfaction, loyalty, and ultimately, long-term success.

Chapter 12

Scaling and Growth Strategies

Scaling and Growth Strategies play a crucial role in the success of any business, regardless of its size or industry. These strategies involve identifying growth opportunities and expansion plans, managing risks and challenges, building strategic partnerships and collaborations, and promoting continuous learning and improvement.

1. Identifying Growth Opportunities and Expansion Plans:

The first step towards scaling and achieving sustainable growth is identifying growth opportunities and defining expansion plans. This involves conducting market research to understand customer needs and demands, analyzing industry trends, and identifying untapped market segments. By identifying growth opportunities, businesses can align their resources and efforts towards expanding their reach and increase their market share. It may involve entering new markets, launching innovative products or services, or diversifying into related industries.

2. Managing Risks and Challenges of Scaling:

Scaling a business can introduce various risks and challenges that need to be addressed effectively. As a business grows, its operational complexities increase, putting pressure on resources, systems, and processes. To manage these risks, businesses need to implement robust risk management strategies, such as conducting regular risk assessments, actively monitoring market trends, and implementing contingency plans. Additionally, businesses need to ensure they have the necessary human resources and infrastructure to support the increased demand and maintain customer satisfaction.

3. Building Strategic Partnerships and Collaborations:

Strategic partnerships and collaborations can significantly contribute to the growth and scalability of a business. By partnering with other businesses or industry experts, companies can tap into their expertise, resources, and networks to accelerate growth. Strategic partnerships can range from joint ventures and co-branding initiatives to distribution agreements and technology alliances. These partnerships can provide access to new markets, technology advancements, and complimentary skill sets, enabling businesses to achieve growth and expand their customer base.

4. Continuous Learning and Improvement:

Scaling and growth strategies should be accompanied by a culture of continuous learning and improvement. Businesses need to encourage their employees to continuously upgrade their skills and knowledge to stay ahead of the competition and adapt to changing market dynamics. It is important to foster a culture of innovation and encourage employees to think outside the box and propose new ideas for improvement. By promoting continuous learning and improvement, businesses can enhance their competitiveness, streamline operations, and refine their products or services to better meet customer demands.

Scaling and growth strategies are essential for businesses to achieve sustainable growth and stay competitive in today's dynamic business landscape. Identifying growth opportunities, managing risks, building strategic partnerships, and promoting continuous learning and improvement are key elements of successful scaling strategies. By adopting these strategies, businesses can effectively navigate the challenges of growth, seize new opportunities, and position themselves for long-term success.

Conclusion

Recap of Key Points:

Starting your own company can be an exciting and rewarding venture, but it's important to approach it with careful planning and preparation. In this guide, we've covered several crucial points to consider when launching your own company.

First and foremost, it's essential to research and identify a viable business idea that aligns with your skills, passions, and market demands. Conduct a thorough market analysis to understand your target audience, competitors, and potential growth opportunities.

Next, create a solid business plan that outlines your objectives, strategies, and financial projections. Your business plan will serve as a roadmap for the future and help you attract investors or secure financing if needed.

When it comes to branding, ensure that your company's name, logo, and messaging accurately reflect your vision and resonate with your target audience. Building a professional website and establishing a strong online presence through social media platforms are key components of a successful launch.

Final Tips and Advice for Success:

To increase your chances of success, it's crucial to surround yourself with a talented and dedicated team. Hiring employees who share your vision and possess the necessary skills will contribute to your company's growth and success.

As you launch your company, it's essential to establish strong relationships with suppliers, partners, and potential customers. Building a network of support and collaboration will not only provide valuable resources but also help you navigate through challenges and open doors to new opportunities.

Financial management is another critical aspect of starting a company. Keep a close eye on your finances, maintain accurate records, and develop a strong understanding of budgeting and cash flow management. Consider seeking advice from professionals or enlisting the help of an accountant to ensure sound financial practices.

Encouragement and Motivation for the Journey Ahead:

Embarking on the journey of launching your own company can be daunting, but remember that many successful entrepreneurs have faced similar challenges and persevered. Embrace the inevitable setbacks and failures as learning opportunities, and stay resilient and persistent in pursuing your goals.

Surround yourself with a support system of mentors, fellow entrepreneurs, and like-minded individuals who can provide guidance, advice, and inspiration along the way. Join business networks, attend industry events, and participate in workshops or conferences to broaden your knowledge and expand your network.

Stay motivated and focused on your vision, regularly revisiting your goals and purpose. Celebrate even the smallest victories and milestones, as they reflect progress and affirm your commitment to your business.

Launching your own company is a thrilling and fulfilling endeavor. By diligently applying the key points covered in this guide, following the provided tips, and maintaining a positive mindset, you are setting yourself up for success. Recall that Rome wasn't created overnight, so exercise perseverance and patience. Your hard work and dedication will pay off as you witness your company grow and thrive in the competitive business world.

Believe in yourself, stay determined, and enjoy the journey ahead!

www.ingramcontent.com/pod-product-compliance
Lightning Source LLC
Chambersburg PA
CBHW071011260726
48661CB00007B/2899